The Wild Young Desert

text and photographs by Ann Atwood

Charles Scribner's Sons/New York

To E. B. H.

who pushed the sun up over the dark dunes

J
910.02
A

B-8.71 [RZ]

Printed in the United States of America

SBN #684–12625–7

Library of Congress Catalog Card Number 73–106536

The Wild Young Desert

After the oceans and the swamps, the mountains and lakes and rain forests, came the desert, the last to inherit the land.

For a desert to be born there must be water and wind and great upheavals in the earth's crust. But most of all there must be a span of time—time whose total overwhelms the mind. Generations upon generations of men could live long lives and disappear while a desert remained in its infancy.

Yet there are deserts which are already old. Aged and quiet now, they flow in gentle waves of sand dissolving into far distances. But most of the earth's deserts are still young, and young deserts are warped with wildness.

81897

Some, born during explosions of earth and tossed up between tilted rocks and lakes and mountains, still tremble with creation.

Robbed of water by the newly formed mountains that empty the rain clouds, the lakes dry up and the land becomes bare. Once created, a desert enters the inevitable cycle of growth and change.

Water

Although it is the absence of water that makes a
desert, it is water that plays the greatest role
in its final shaping. The land, no longer pro-
tected by a covering of green growth, is gnawed
level by the melting snows and sudden rains, and
sawed into narrow canyons by strong rivers that
well up from subterranean springs.

These rivers whittle steep gorges out of giant blocks of stone.

Fierce, infrequent rains join the snow-streams from above and the
river water from below to etch the terraces down into wrinkled cones.

But their work is often stamped with grandeur as they carve domed mosques with flaming minarets; or rake away the soft sand beneath a shelf of harder rock, leaving a sphinx-like pyramid to guard the flatlands.

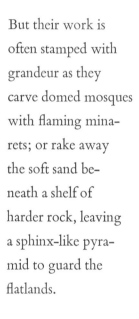

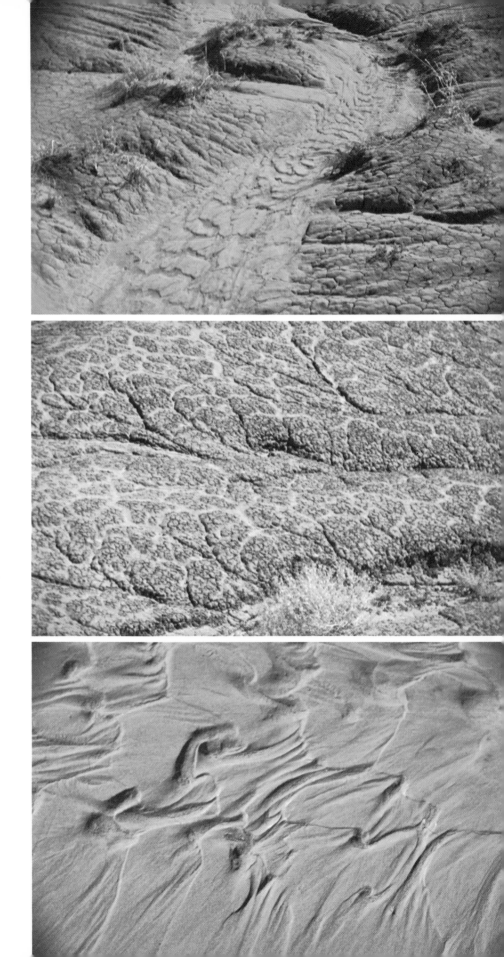

Wherever water moves
or has moved there is
rhythmic design. In
the narrow hollows of
withered streams are
patterns of desolate
beauty.

Even among the ruins
of ancient lake-beds
whose waters turned
to salt thousands of
years ago, crystals
that look like snow-
flakes sparkle on the
desert floor. Hidden
here is a miniature
arctic world of gleam-
ing cut-glass pools
and ice palaces, and
fjords with frozen
waterfalls.

Wind

Once a desert is roughly shaped there is little to hinder the wind. It races over the wastelands gathering strength, smoothing the jagged contours left by the rivers and rains. It sweeps the crumbling terraces clean of loose sediments and, grinding these into velvet sand, rolls them into textured dunes.

It is the rippling, savage wind that softens the scarred moonscape of the wild young desert.

The tapering mesas, the gentle hillocks of sandstone, the undulating furrows of rock, these are the curving patterns of the wind.

They are repeated in the rounded columns of cliffs and in the smallest particle of sand. There is power as well as symmetry in this circular design. Tumbled by wind, a grain of granite is chipped and ground to an almost weightless sphere, so indestructible that it can travel across continents and survive for a million years!

There are grains not light enough to be carried away and yet not heavy enough to be left on the ground. The wind churns these into a sea of sand and drives the cresting waves mile after mile.

Life

Yet even in this wilderness, devastated by
wind and flood and shifting sands, life
appears. After a brief season of rainfall
the parched and colorless floor of the desert explodes in green splendor, as seeds,
long-buried, stir out of a safe sleep.

Unique plants, having adapted to a land of
little soil and even less water, gather and
store the vital rain into trunks and branches
which they guard with spiney thorns. This
inner reservoir will have to last through
the months of drought ahead.

There are a few shrubs that send down long, streaming roots to underground sources of water. These can afford the luxury of thirsty leaves. But most plants spend all the nourishment they can hoard on their blossoms, whose brilliant glory must entice the pollinating insects and whose fruit will carry the seeds of continuing life.

It is this vegetation alone that makes
other life on the desert possible.
Clusters of cactuses form screened
enclosures where tiny animals can rest.

The many plants, flowers, fruits and
seeds supply a vast community of living
things with food and water and insu-
lated nests.

In this arid, hostile country no creature could survive without
the shelter of a shadow in which to take refuge until the cool
of evening.

All growth is a shield between the earth and the searing sun,
creating a world in which countless creatures live and thrive
and reproduce their kind.

Beneath this life-filled desert world lies another world, forgotten, but very much present. Every thimbleful of earth is crowded with atoms of some being which once shared this same place on the planet. There is only a slender chance that any part of these life-forms could be preserved, and all but impossible that any could still remain whole. Yet this chambered nautilus lived here a hundred million years ago—in a time when this desert belonged to the sea.

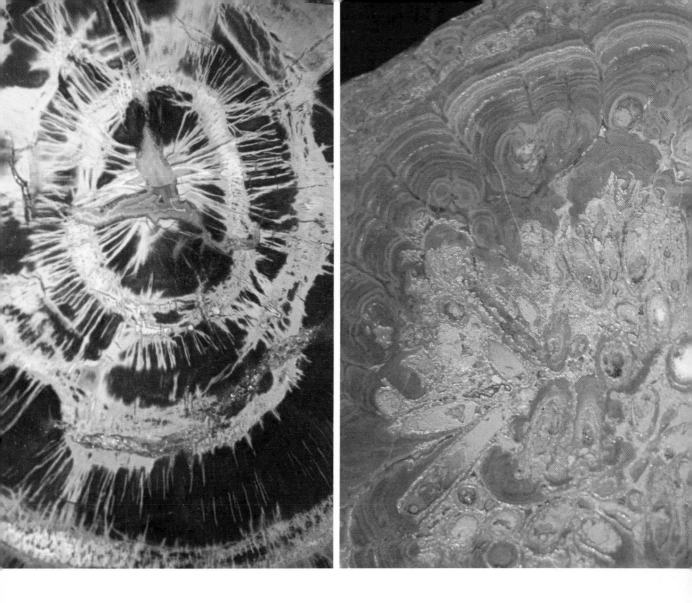

Because of this miracle of preservation, we can see into the hearts
of the first flowering plants to appear on this earth and hold in
our hands a jewelled section of their primitive fruit.

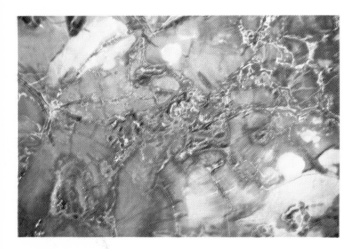

Before the sea there were swamps here where dinosaurs roamed
among giant ferns and trees and groves of pines. Millions of years
ago, at the time when great mountains rose, some of these trees
were shoved upward and hurled about. Wind and rain washed
away the soil in which they were encased and left their bare trunks
lying on the desert floor. Gradually they were turned to stone by
tremendous pressures and by in-flowing water whose minerals
transformed them into quartz and agate, amethyst and jasper.

In geologic time a thousand years is but a day, and in these lengthened days many things can happen to change a youthful desert. The sharp blade of a river may cut its red mesas in half and its walls may be leveled by eroding wind and rain, until eventually it ages into a tranquil plain. And so it grows old.

Or mountains that stole the moisture from the clouds may sink, or distant icecaps melt so that water pours back into the land. Then the rising forests will send their green armies clambering over the sandstone castles to conquer the arid kingdom. And so the desert vanishes.

Or, as many times before, when gigantic spasms of earth upend the cliffs and canyons, creating bold land-forms, steep mountains may leap up to capture the rain.

So in a new dawn the desert will be born again, young and wild, once more untamed by wind and water.